transformed
living
in
tough times

DEVOTIONS

Also by John Ed Mathison

Transformed Living in Tough Times
Transformed Giving
Treasures of the Transformed Life
Extra Effort
Fishing for Birds
Every Member in Ministry

transformed living *in* tough times

by John Ed Mathison

DEVOTIONS

Abingdon Press
Nashville

Transformed Living in Tough Times
Devotions

Copyright © 2010 by Abingdon Press

Library of Congress Cataloging-in-Publication Data

Mathison, John Ed.
Transformed living in tough times : devotions / by John Ed Mathison.
    p. cm.
ISBN 978-0-687-66032-2 (pbk./trade pbk. : alk. paper)
1. Suffering—Prayers and devotions. 2. Struggle—Prayers and devotions.
I. Title.
BV283.S84M38 2010
242'.4—dc22

2010022187

10 11 12 13 14 15 16 17 18 19 — 10 9 8 7 6 5 4 3 2 1
MANUFACTURED IN THE UNITED STATES OF AMERICA

Contents

Introduction

Today, when we speak of tough times, our first thought goes to the economic downslide that our country has recently experienced. All of us have felt the effect of those tough times; however, this book and its companion *Transformed Living in Tough Times* address more than economic factors.

Tough times come in all areas of life—finances, health concerns, family issues, natural disasters, and more. When factors seem beyond our control, we can develop feelings of helplessness, anger, and depression, or we can allow God to lift us to a new level of faith and living.

People of faith—transformed people—experience tough times, sometimes more than others; however, we have the ability to rise above the storm and handle tough times effectively.

Transformed Living in Tough Times: Devotions contains sixty short motivations to help you keep your focus on God and rise above the storm of tough times. Use these devotions to begin your day on a high note, or read and meditate on them at the end of a tough day.

Focusing on four practical elements of navigating tough times—return to priorities, focus on fundamentals, exercise God's creativity, and develop a Christlike attitude—this book works well when read alone or along with *Transformed Living in Tough Times*.

1
Lift Your Feet

"For God so loved the world that he gave his only Son, so that everyone who believes in him may not perish but may have eternal life." (John 3:16, NRSV)

 missionary was working in another country, translating the New Testament into a cultural language. He had been working on translating John 3:16. "For God so loved the world that he gave his only Son, so that everyone who . . ." What? "Believes." He couldn't come up with an appropriate cultural term for *belief*.

The missionary took his problem to one of the local men. He asked the man, "What is belief?"

The man said, "Well, what are you doing?"

"Right now? I'm sitting in a chair," the missionary replied.

The man said, "Are your feet are on the ground?"

"Yes. That's right."

"Lift your feet," the man directed.

The missionary did as instructed and lifted his feet.

The man nodded his head and said, "Now, what are you doing?"

"I'm putting my whole weight on the chair," the missionary replied.

"That's what faith is," said the man.

The missionary was then able to complete the translation of John 3:16.

Faith is when you put your whole weight on who God is in Jesus Christ.

F—orsaking

A—ll

I

T—ake

H—im

The transformed person focuses on how much he or she is worth to God, not to the world. We are worth everything to him. We are worth so much that he sent his only son into the world so that whosoever believes in him should never perish but have everlasting life.

Father, my God; I praise your name. You have done marvelous things, things that you planned long ago. Hold me up as I put my whole faith in you and you alone.

2
Hold My Hand

"He goes ahead of them, and the sheep follow him because they know his voice." (John 10:4b, NRSV)

n 2010, just as in biblical times, a shepherd spends many hours every day with his sheep. In fact, he spends so much time with his sheep that the sheep learn to identify his voice. When sheep hear their shepherd talking, and see him with a staff, they have a sense of security. They know that everything will be OK.

When I was young, my family lived in Wetumpka, Alabama. My dad was a preacher there, and we lived next door to the church. I remember when I was around six years old, maybe younger, Dad would ask me to go over to the church and get a book, some papers, or something like that for him. It was always at night, and that big old dark church was scary to me. The light switches were not always easy to find, and I didn't like going in there by myself.

Have you ever been in a dark church by yourself? Every time there's the slightest little sound, you can imagine all sorts of things.

You know what I'd always say when Dad asked me to go over there in the dark? "Daddy, you go with me." If he walked over there with me, I wasn't afraid at all. When we went through the door together, you know what I'd do. I'd reach up and grab his hand. If I held my Daddy's hand, I'd go anywhere. I knew he would take care of me.

Transformed people have the same relationship with the Holy Father. When we are scared, we can ask him to go with us. We can reach up and hold his hand. We can be assured that he will take care of us—everything will be OK.

Heavenly Father, when I hear your voice, I know everything is OK. I rejoice in the shadow of your wings. Thank you for holding my hand.

3
Money Doesn't Give Happiness

" 'I know! I'll tear down my barns and build bigger ones. Then I'll have room enough to store all my wheat and other goods. And I'll sit back and say to myself, "My friend, you have enough stored away for years to come. Now take it easy! Eat, drink, and be merry!" But God said to him, 'You fool! You will die this very night. Then who will get everything you worked for?' Yes, a person is a fool to store up earthly wealth but not have a rich relationship with God." (Luke 12:18-21, NLT)

 od understands profit differently from us. Luke 12 records a story Jesus told that shows us what profit means in God's economics. When the very successful farmer gathered his crop, his barns were not sufficient to hold the harvest. So the farmer reasoned, "Here's what I'll do: I'll tear down my barns and build bigger ones. Then I'll gather in all my grain and goods, and I'll say to

myself, Self, you've done well! You've got it made and can now retire. Take it easy and have the time of your life!" (The Message). Notice how many times personal pronouns are used.

By human economics standards, the man needed bigger barns. But God's economics is different. God came to the man and told him that he was a fool. He asked, when you die, this very night, who will get everything that you worked for? Then, Jesus drove home the message by agreeing that only a fool will store up earthly wealth and not have a rich relationship with God.

The world thinks that if we can just have a little more, we will be happy. A lot of folks are working long hours and some people take second jobs just so the family can get more things.

Let me tell you, money—the love of money—becomes the root of all evil. Take a look at John D. Rockefeller. After he died, people asked his accountant just how much money Rockefeller left behind. The accountant's answer? "All of it; every cent of it. He didn't take a bit of money with him."

Lord, you are my strength, the reason for my song. Majestic and holy! Fearsome and glorious! Miracle worker! I praise and honor you.

4

Leave the
Pigpen Behind

*"After he had gone through all his money, there was a bad
famine all through that country and he began to hurt. . . . He
was so hungry he would have eaten the corncobs in the pig
slop, but no one would give him any." (Luke 15:14-16,
The Message)*

esus told a story about a man who had two
sons. One son worked hard, put in a full
day's work every day. But the other son had
lofty ideas. He came up with what he
thought was a better financial plan than
what his father had.

The son with lofty ideas talked his father into giving him
his inheritance, and then he went out to seek his fortune.
He focused on the wilds of the earthly life and of course,
his plan quickly became a disaster. He unintentionally lost
every cent he was given. He ended up working for a farmer,
slopping pigs.

This wasn't his plan. He didn't set out to wind up in a pigpen, but he did. Misaligned priorities—focusing on earthly ways—always lead to a pigpen. The good news is that the prodigal son "came to his senses" (Luke15:17, NLT). He woke up and began to think rationally.

The best part of the story is that the boy's father was already looking for him. He was ready to take his son back into his home.

In tough times, when transformed people consciously decide to leave life's pigpens and return home, we find our Heavenly Father is already waiting for us with open arms.

Lord, my God, thank you for keeping me going while times are tough. You are my bedrock. You are my hope.

5
Acres of Diamonds

"What profit is it to a man if he gains the whole world, and loses his own soul?" (Matthew 16:26, NKJV)

man named Russell Conwell made millions of dollars making a speech. He went all over the world talking about "Acres of Diamonds." He told a story about a farmer who wanted to find the finest diamonds in the world. The farmer sold his farm and used the money to travel around the world looking for the best diamonds.

You know how the story goes. The farmer never found the very best diamonds. He squandered his money, searching for sparkle and glitz. He ended his voyage sad and broke. He went back to his little hometown only to discover that the man who had bought his farm had discovered one of the richest veins of diamonds ever found.

Now, here that farmer had gone around the world and

spent all of his money looking for what he had had all the time.

You know, you can go through life looking for happiness—and spend a great deal of money searching for it too—but I want to tell you, it's right in your back pocket. It's right where you are. God has given everything to you and me that he wants us to have in order to accomplish the plan and purpose he has for us.

Lord, I am joyful and glad in heart for the good things that you have done for me. You have given me cause to rejoice over tough times.

6
Storing Treasures

*"Don't store up treasures here on earth, where moths eat
them and rust destroys them, and where thieves break in
and steal. Store your treasures in heaven, where moths and
rust cannot destroy, and thieves do not break in and steal.
Wherever your treasure is, there the desires of your heart
will also be." (Matthew 6:19-21, NLT)*

e're living in a world of persuasion. We're
living in a world where sales and market-
ing influence our decisions. The reason we
buy the clothing that we do, the reason we
invest in expensive jewelry and the latest
cars, is that we are tuned into commercials. We buy things
we don't need because someone is a good salesperson. What
we are actually being sold is a bill of goods. People who are
good at selling are persuading us to buy things we can't af-
ford and don't even really want.

I read about a fellow who stopped at a little one-room

country store. The man saw boxes of salt lined up on every wall and on every shelf. He turned to the storeowner and said, "Man, you must sell a lot of salt." The storeowner said, "Not so much, but there was a guy through here a few days ago who could really sell the stuff."

We are all victims of persuasive arguments. We fall far short of what God wants us to be and do because we become deceived by persuasive arguments. Transformed people must allow the Lord Jesus Christ to call the shots. We need to focus on heavenly treasures and forego the persuasive arguments that bombard us every day. God's economics deals with this life and for eternity. If we lay up our treasures in heaven, we have invested our time and energy and resources wisely.

Heavenly Father, you know the desires of my heart. Close my ears to the persuasive arguments of earthly things. Help me keep my eyes focused on you.

7
Transcending Tough Times

Your attitude should be the same as that of Christ Jesus.
(Philippians 2:5, NIV)

or any situation that transformed people face, there are two choices. We can see the issue as either a problem or an opportunity. When you search the Bible, you will find that the folks who trusted in God never saw problems, they only saw possibilities.

A little boy was in the backyard tossing a softball in the air and hitting at it with his bat. His dad went outside and asked, "Son, what are you doing?"

The boy replied, "Dad, I'm the greatest hitter in the world!" As he spoke, he tossed the ball in the air, swung his bat, and missed the ball.

The boy's father said, "Son, you are not the greatest hitter in the world."

Again, the boy tossed the ball in the air, swung, and

missed. "Yes, Daddy. I am the greatest hitter in the world!" he said.

"No, Son. You are not the greatest hitter in the world," the father continued.

"Well then, I'm the greatest pitcher in the world," the boy said as he again tossed the ball in the air.

The Carnegie Institute did a study, interviewing successful people in all phases of life, and came up with an interesting conclusion. The researchers discovered that for successful people, only 15 percent of their success is due to talent and ability. The other 85 percent is due to attitude.

Probably the most important thing transformed people face is not the situation itself, but their attitude toward it. For every one of us, there are some mountaintops and some valleys, but our attitudes toward those situations are far more important than the situations themselves. The attitude that will help us transcend tough times is the attitude that Jesus had.

Father, I don't understand your purpose, but I trust in your name with all my heart. I pray that you will keep my path straight and my feet from stumbling. Lead me beside still waters and keep me from evil.

8
Power Up With God

"With God everything is possible." (Matthew 19:26b, NLT)

 college professor wanted to show his class the immense power of a growing squash. The professor took a common yellow squash and hooked a harness and a scale to it. The object was that as the squash grew, it would pull against the harness, and the scale would measure how much growing power—pulling power—the squash was producing.

After a couple of days, the students returned to class and found that the little squash had started to grow. It pulled 5 pounds, then 10 pounds and then 20 pounds. In just a short time, the squash pulled 100 pounds. Then it pulled 500 pounds. The students—and even the professor, if the truth was told—couldn't believe that the common yellow squash like they loved to eat during the summertime could pull 1,000 pounds, and even 2,000 pounds!

Then one night, some vandals broke into the classroom, and with one sharp swoosh with a knife, cut the vine leading to the squash. You know what happened. That scale went down to zero. The squash no longer had any pulling power. It was no longer connected to its source of strength. When the vine that was giving it the power—the nutrition—to pull was cut, the scale went down to zero.

Now let me tell you about your life and mine. If we are connected to God, his power can allow us to do some awesome things. There's nothing that God can't do—everything is possible through him. If a little yellow squash can pull thousands of pounds when connected to its power source, just think of the amazing things that we as transformed people can do when we are connected to our power source—God.

Heavenly Father, I cannot face today alone. I need you to be my power source. I know that only by your power can I do that which must be done today.

9
Walking the Talk

"A man had two sons, and he came to the first and said, 'Son, go, work today in my vineyard.' He answered and said, 'I will not,' but afterward he regretted it and went. Then he came to the second and said likewise. And he answered and said, 'I go, sir,' but he did not go. Which of the two did the will of his father?" (Matthew 21:28-31, NKJV)

esus told a parable about a man who had two sons. The man asked both sons to go to work in his business. One son said: "Sure, Dad, I would be glad to go to work. I look forward to working in your business." But then, he didn't do anything. On the other hand, the man's other son had a different attitude. He was honest with his father. He said, "Dad, I don't care about working for you." Later on, the son changed his mind and went to work in his dad's business.

Which of the sons do you think responded appropriately?

Which one earned the father's respect? The son who said he didn't want to work in his father's business, and then later on changed his mind, spoke honestly. His father could trust him to do the work that he had agreed to do. That young man, although at first he may not given the answer his father wanted to hear, had integrity. The other son said the right words but was unreliable.

In God's economics, collateral is commitment with integrity. It is obedience. It is not just talking the talk, but walking the walk. One of the crucial things about living in tough times is whether or not we are willing to do things God's way or our way.

Dear Lord, remove my selfish ways and help me to respond to tough times with integrity. Lead me today as I strive to walk in the pathway you have laid out for me.

10
Take a Risk

For God has not given us a spirit of fear, but of power and of love and of a sound mind. (2 Timothy 1:7, NKJV)

 turtle never gets in trouble until he sticks his neck out; and you never stump your toe when you're standing still. I'm not much for standing still. I'd rather be moving forward in God's direction.

One of our nation's greatest businessmen was Charles Kettering. Much of modern technology is a result of some of the things he dreamed. In fact, he is the person who developed the first electrical ignition system for cars. It is because of Mr. Kettering that you and I don't have to get out every morning and use a hand crank to get our cars started.

Kettering used his imagination and wanted others to do so too. Whenever he had a meeting with his executives, he would take up all the gadgets—slide rules, adding machines, and calculators (if anybody had one), and leave them outside the meeting room. He knew that as soon as the group came up with a great idea one of them would pull out a gadget, add up the cost, and say, "Boss, let me show you why this plan won't work." Just imagine what he would think about today's smart phones!

Let me suggest that you put the calculators and smart phones outside the door. Let's dream God's dream. We don't need to analyze and criticize and build stumbling blocks. We only need to have faith and follow God. He did not give transformed people a sense of fear. Instead, he gave us power, love, and a sound mind.

Lord, there are no calculators or smart phones that have the answers I need today. Only you have the answers for me to traverse these troubled times. Open my ears and let me hear your voice. Guide me so that I may dream your dreams.

11
Our Weakness Is God's Strength

But he [God] replied, "My kindness is all you need. My power is strongest when you are weak." So if Christ keeps giving me his power, I will gladly brag about how weak I am. Yes, I am glad to be weak or insulted or mistreated or to have troubles and sufferings, if it is for Christ. Because when I am weak, I am strong. (2 Corinthians 12:9-10, CEV)

aul was glad to be weak, mistreated, and have troubles. Now, we don't usually hear people expressing gladness over their weakness. More often, we're told to be strong. We are encouraged to be the biggest, the best, and carry the most weight. But that's a worldly way of thinking, not what the Bible tells us.

Paul said, "When I am weak, I am strong." He understood the importance of relying on God when tough times came his way. As he admitted his own weakness and stepped out of God's way, he allowed God to work through him. It was not Paul's human ability but God's tremendous strength that took over and triumphed in tough times.

In 1652, at age 44, poet John Milton lost his eyesight. Sudden blindness stops many people in their tracks, but Milton acknowledged his weakness and stepped out of the way. He continued to write by composing verses at night in his head, memorizing them, and then dictating them to his aides each morning. He did this for fifteen years and completed what has been called one of the greatest works written in the English language—*Paradise Lost*. In a similar manner, he continued to write for the rest of his life. *History of Britain* was published in 1670; *Paradise Regained* and *Samson Agonistes* were published in 1671. And six years later, only months before his death, the second edition of *Paradise Lost* was published. Because Milton allowed God's strength to take over in light of his weakness, his writing continues to inspire people nearly four hundred years later.

We're good at conquering our world, aren't we? We think we're good at coming out on top intellectually or financially or with more power. You know what Jesus said about our desire for strength and control. The person who submits to God is the one who has real strength. It is in our weakness that we find strength.

Father, forgive me for standing in your way. Give me the courage to admit to my weakness and praise you for it.

12
Tough Times Strengthen Our Character

We also glory in tribulations, knowing that tribulation produces perseverance; and perseverance, character; and character, hope. Now hope does not disappoint, because the love of God has been poured out in our hearts by the Holy Spirit who was given to us. (Romans 5:3-5, NKJV)

verybody will have tribulation. Trials and troubles are going to come. I can promise you, you're going to have some tribulations.

Tribulation comes from the word *tribulum*, a farming instrument used in New Testament days. A *tribulum*, simply a rope tied to a stick, was used in harvesting wheat. When the wheat was ripe, a farmer would take the rope and hit the wheat stalks. The *tribulum* jarred the stalks, causing the chaff, which was no good, to fly off. Then the wind would blow the chaff away, and the good seed, the wheat, would fall to the ground.

The *tribulum* was what separated the good from the use-

31

less. Isn't that a great concept? When transformed people have tribulation, the intent is to separate the useless from what's good and healthy and wholesome.

Have you ever watched a jeweler chip away at a diamond's rough edges? Or a metalsmith who burns away the impurities of fine metals? We all have probably watched a farmer plowing, turning a field, disturbing the weeds, and revealing the rich soil beneath. This is what God does when he walks with us through tribulation—tough times. Yes, he is walking with transformed people all the time, even guiding our every move. We need not be afraid of our tribulation; we need only remember that God is preparing us so that his glory will shine through us.

Your tribulation, the trouble you face, may be strong stalks, or it might be a snake. I don't know how big your tribulation will be, but I can say every one of us is going to face troubles, trials, and tribulation. It is up to you to glory in your tribulation, knowing that God is strengthening your character, preparing you for a great work that he wants to accomplish through you.

Heavenly Father, prepare me for the tribulation that is to come. Break away my chaff and reveal the good and healthy and wholesome within me. Pour your love into my heart during tough times.

13

The Lord Instructs Us in What to Say

But Moses pleaded with the LORD, "O Lord, I'm not very good with words. I never have been, and I'm not now, even though you have spoken to me. I get tongue-tied, and my words get tangled." Then the LORD asked Moses, 'Who makes a person's mouth? Who decides whether people speak or do not speak, hear or do not hear, see or do not see? Is it not I, the LORD? Now go! I will be with you as you speak, and I will instruct you in what to say." (Exodus 4:10-12, NLT)

 hen God wanted to lead his children out of Israel, he picked Moses to be his leader. Now Moses started making excuses. God asked him to do something, and he started making excuses for why he couldn't do it. For every excuse that he came up with, God said, "Moses, that's not your problem; it's mine. You let me handle it. If you are obedient to me, I will supply everything that you need."

If God calls us to do something, our only task is to be

obedient. It's his responsibility to supply everything that we need to do that specific task. We simply are to trust and obey.

There's a story about a young woman who was comfortable working with computers and developed a passion for teaching others to use them. After reading about women in her community who needed job skills training, she decided to open a computer training business. She took business classes at the local college, and even spoke with her pastor about her plans. As a matter of fact, she talked about her plans quite a bit with her friends and family. But, that's as far as it went. You see, she never pursued a new business start-up loan or a building for her business. She said that she just wasn't good with words. She was afraid that she would get tongue-tied, and her words would get tangled. And besides, she thought, they wouldn't listen to her or believe her. We can only guess what might have been accomplished if this young woman had trusted God to provide the words for her.

When transformed people team with Jesus and walk with him, we cannot help but be successful. We actually discover that even during tough times, life is meaningful and purposeful. Team with Jesus; he is a faithful partner.

Dear Lord, I am relying on you today. Give me the words you want me to say and the courage to say them to the people you place in my path.

14

A Leap of Faith

He poured water into a basin and began to wash the disciples' feet, and to wipe them with the towel with which He was girded. Then He came to Simon Peter. And Peter said to Him, "Lord, are You washing my feet?" Jesus answered and said to him, "What I am doing you do not understand now, but you will know after this." (John 13:5-7, NKJV)

 esus took the disciples a basin of water and a rag, then started washing their feet. Immediately Peter said, "Lord, what are you doing?" Jesus said to Peter, "You can't understand that."

God doesn't ask us to understand what is happening; he simply asks us to obey. Jesus said to Peter, "Look, Peter, you don't know what I'm doing, but you just do what I do and serve as I am serving."

The South African sharp-nosed grass frog is an interesting little frog. It only grows to be about two-and-a-half inches long. But one of these little frogs holds the world record for jumping. It jumped 10.3 meters—that's 33 feet, 10 inches! But do you know an interesting fact about these frogs? They don't have to be tied down to keep them from jumping. All a person has to do is put a little piece of cardboard about a foot-and-a-half high in front of the frog. The frog will not jump unless it can see where it's going to land. Behind a foot-and-a-half wall, he won't jump because he can't see.

You know what fear says: "I'm not going to move unless I can see exactly where you're leading me." It takes faith to venture into what we cannot see. Transformed people don't need the evidence of things not seen. We're willing to take a leap of faith. We don't need to know God's plan. All we need to do is follow him—do what he is doing.

Lord, I feel like I have a cardboard barrier in front of me. I am afraid to venture out into the tough times that are ahead of me. Erase my fear. Help me to make the leap of faith.

15
The Perfect House

God, your love is so precious! You protect people in the shadow of your wings. They eat the rich food in your house, and you let them drink from your river of pleasure. You are the giver of life. Your light lets us enjoy life. (Psalm 36:7-9, NCV)

 husband and wife called a real estate agent and told him to sell their house. "Write it up and put it in the paper tomorrow," they directed. The next morning, the couple began scanning the paper, looking for another house to move into. At the same time, they both spotted the perfect ad. The more they read, the better the house sounded. They called the phone number and told the real estate agent this was the house they were looking for.

They drove across town, met with the real estate agent, and got into his car. The agent drove the couple back across town, all the while telling them about the wonderful house they were going to see.

Now, you know what? They pulled up in front of their own house.

Do you know that most of us sit around and say everything would be better if something was different? We would like a situation if it would be this way or that, but not the way it is. However, if we would look at life from God's perspective, we'd discover that the situation is exactly the way God designed it to be.

What does your house look like? Would it be the perfect house if you saw an ad for it in the newspaper? What about other parts of your life? A lot about our happiness and success is based on the way we look at things—our perspective.

Father, you are my strength. Your word is sufficient for me. Turn my focus on you and away from earthly desires.

16
One Man's Scraps

"It's God's Spirit in a person, the breath of the Almighty One, that makes wise human insight possible." (Job 32:8, The Message)

 have a good friend, Mike Henig, who lives in Montgomery, Alabama. He serves as Chairman of the Board of the John Ed Mathison Leadership Ministries. Mike is in the fur business. The material that his company uses to make coats is quite valuable, so their cutting methods are precise. However, Mike had noticed that a few scraps were always left over from making the coats. Instead of throwing the scraps away, he decided to sew them together and make little teddy bears out of them.

Mike liked the little teddy bears so much that he kept one and put it in his office. He had that little scrap teddy bear in his office when a leading manufacturing representative from Arkansas came by to talk business. At the end of the visit, Mike showed the man the teddy bear. The man said, "Oh, we wouldn't have a market for that." You know what Mike's response was? Instead of seeing the man's response as an obstacle, Mike gave him the teddy bear. He said, "Well, if you ever want some of them, let me know."

The man returned to Arkansas. The next day the scrap teddy bear was on the corner of the man's desk when his boss—Sam Walton, the founder of Wal-Mart—came in. Mr. Walton picked up the teddy bear and said, "I really like that. Order us 10,000."

Now, creative thinking turned scraps into teddy bears, and seeing an opportunity instead of an obstacle turned a rejection into an order for 10,000 little teddy bears. That was the initial order.

Lord, breathe in me your wisdom. I seek your holy guidance for the tough times ahead. Lead me, guide me, and let your wisdom show through me.

17
A Good Root System

"A sower went out to sow. And as he sowed, some seeds fell
. . . on rocky ground, where they did not have much soil,
and they sprang up quickly, since they had no depth of soil.
But when the sun rose, they were scorched; and since they
had no root, they withered away. . . . Other seeds fell on
good soil and brought forth grain, some a hundredfold,
some sixty, some thirty. Let anyone with ears listen!"
(Matthew 13:3-9, NRSV)

esus once told a story about a man who
went out with seeds to scatter. He threw
the seeds out, and they fell on all different
kinds of soil. The seeds that fell on hard soil
didn't do so well. The little seeds pene-
trated the soil, but they couldn't go very deep and form a
good root system. Those seeds grew stems and leaves.
Eventually, the part of the plants above ground—what the
farmer could see—looked healthy. But as soon as the sun

came up, the little plants suffered. They had no root system to rely on.

Jesus said it is essential that our root systems grow deep. Look at any tree. The higher a tree grows, the deeper its root system must go into the ground to give it nourishment and stability.

One night we had a little storm in east Montgomery, where I live. When I went out to get into the car and go to church, I noticed that one of my neighbor's trees had fallen. The whole tree was uprooted. I could see the roots were not very long at all. Just a little wind blew the tree completely over. It had no root system to anchor it into the ground.

When the winds and stress of life blow against you, are you going to fall over? When you find yourself in a tough situation, do you have the root system to make a wise decision or to react appropriately? Are you firmly rooted in Jesus Christ?

Lord, I have ears. I am listening for your voice. Teach me to make decisions, to react the way you want me to react.

18
Living Life

Love the Lord *your God with all your heart, soul, and strength . . . . obey his laws and worship him with fear and trembling. And if we do, he will protect us and help us be successful. (Deuteronomy 6:5, 25, CEV)*

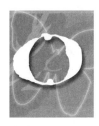ne day a man received a birthday card from his young grandson. The little boy had written a note on the bottom of the card: "Granddaddy, I hope you live all of your life." Although the boy got his words mixed up, he had a wise message for his grandfather.

So many folks don't live all of their lives. They allow worry and problems and resentment and grudges to steal the days away from them.

When Moses was speaking to the children of Israel in Deuteronomy 6, they were getting ready to go into the Promised Land. He wanted to say to them that even though they had come through the desert, even though they had encountered all of those hardships, going into the Promised Land wasn't going to be easy either. You see, Moses knew they would face earthly problems even in the Promised Land, but he wanted them to make the most of every day, to obey God, and not yield to temptations.

Look over at the New Testament. Do you see all those letters that the Apostle Paul wrote? He wanted folks to live life. Some of those letters he wrote while sitting in a jail cell. He didn't know how many days he had left, but he wasn't thinking about how short his life was to be or how terrible sitting in jail was. No, he simply wrote to people he knew to encourage them. There he was in jail, encouraging other people, to live life for the Lord.

I wish I could tell you how many days you've got left. In my business, I confront folks each week who thought they had a lot of days ahead of them, but all of a sudden something happens and those days became greatly narrowed. It doesn't matter how many days we have left. What matters is what we do with those days.

Heavenly Father, I want to live today. Share your vision with me. Fill me with your boldness and strength so that I might become your instrument.

19
Noise to the Extreme

The boat by this time was a long way from the land, beaten by the waves, for the wind was against them. And in the fourth watch of the night he came to them, walking on the sea. But when the disciples saw him walking on the sea, they were terrified, and said, "It is a ghost!" and they cried out in fear. But immediately Jesus spoke to them, saying, "Take heart; it is I. Do not be afraid." (Matthew 14:24-27, ESV)

 ave you ever been in a place where it was so noisy that you couldn't think? I was at an Auburn University basketball game one night when they were playing Arkansas, one of the top teams in the nation at that time. A few thousand folks were there watching Auburn make a comeback. As the game was nearing the end, the noise was so loud people could not even hear themselves think. Arkansas had the ball, and the whole team became

disoriented. They couldn't hear each other, their coach, or the referee.

The same kind of thing happened to Jesus' disciples. Late at night, the men were out in their fishing boat and a strong storm came up. There was probably loud thunder; the ocean waves roared and tossed the boat about, and the men became disoriented and frightened. They had become so wrapped up in the storm that Jesus startled them. He was walking out on the water to join them when they cried out in fear.

You know, when the noise and the tension get so extreme, we lose track of what's going on right in front of us. When the noises of life are so loud, we don't hear the Head Coach when he's trying to tell us what to do.

When the noise of tough times gets too loud, tone it down and listen. You can hear Jesus speaking to you, just as the disciples did: "Don't be afraid. Take courage. I am here!"

Father, the noise of tough times is too loud for me today. Please help me turn down the volume. I need to hear your voice, Lord.

20

The Power of God

"Why do you wonder at this, or why do you stare at us, as though by our own power or piety we had made him walk? . . . the faith that is through Jesus has given him this perfect health in the presence of all of you." (Acts 3:12, 16, NRSV)

eter and John came upon a lame beggar one day as they were walking to the temple to pray. The disciples said to him, "We don't have money but we will give you what we do have. We'll be obedient in the name of Jesus. Rise up and walk."

For the first time, the man's legs received strength. He was so overwhelmed with joy that he jumped up and ran around the community. Can you imagine the look on people's faces? Here was the man they had seen day in and day out, unable to stand, unable to work, and now he's jumping around, laughing, and giving them all high-fives. What a sight to behold!

People shouted out to him, "Man, what is happening to you?"

"I don't know—all I did was obey what Peter and John told me to do."

The man went into the temple to offer prayers of thanksgiving, and people surrounded Peter and John. They wanted to know in what name—in what power—they were able to heal the lame man. The disciples responded, "It's only in the power of Jesus, and we're simply obeying him."

A man in Australia was thinking about buying a Rolls Royce. He asked a salesman how much horsepower the engine had. The salesman answered honestly, "They don't ever tell us that, but I will see if I can find out." No one at the dealership knew the answer, so they contacted the manufacturing plant in England to find out how much horsepower is in a Rolls Royce. The response came back in only one word—*sufficient*.

The most powerful thing in the world is the power of the Holy Spirit. How much power will God give you? *Sufficient*.

Heavenly Father, thank you for your sufficient power. Help me to see the opportunities that I have today to tell others about your power.

21
Heavenly Vision

Set your minds on things above, not on earthly things.
(Colossians 3:2, NIV)

I borrowed somebody's glasses to read a little piece of paper. When I put those glasses on, I couldn't see a thing. They gave me a perspective that I'd never had.

Luke 10 tells about two sisters, Martha and Mary, who had very different perspectives. Both women were excited to have their friend Jesus come to visit in their home. Martha set about cleaning the floors and dusting under the chairs. Cooking, cleaning, and offering a comfortable home was Martha's perspective for honoring her very special friend. Mary, on the other hand, focused her attention on Jesus. Instead of helping Martha around the house, she focused on taking care of and listening to Jesus. She actually sat at his feet and hung on every word that he was saying. She knew whatever he had to say was too important to miss by being in the kitchen.

Martha viewed Jesus' visit with earthly eyes, while Mary was using heavenly vision. Martha became exasperated with Mary and asked Jesus to have Mary come and help her with the work. Instead, Jesus commended Mary for her perspective. He said, "My dear Martha, you are worried and upset over all these details! There is only one thing worth being concerned about. Mary has discovered it, and it will not be taken away from her" (Luke 10:41, NLT). Jesus wasn't praising Mary for not helping her sister, nor was he scolding Martha for working around the house. He was expressing the importance of keeping our attention on God and not on earthly things.

God has given transformed people a different perspective. He has given us a new set of glasses. We don't have to look at things with earthly eyes; we have an eternal perspective. And when our perspective changes, our priorities change.

Father, help me take off my earthly glasses and show me your vision. I want to focus on you, not on tough times.

22
Moribundus

A cheerful heart is a good medicine. (Proverbs 17:22a, NRSV)

octor Gordon Allport, a famous psychologist, told the story of a patient in a hospital in Houston, Texas. Many doctors tried hard to find out what was wrong with the patient, but they couldn't make a diagnosis. In the patient's presence, one of the doctors said, "If we can't diagnosis his illness, he's going to die." This caused the patient to become depressed, and his health declined even more.

The next week, one more doctor examined the patient. The doctor turned to the other physicians, again in the presence of the patient, and said, "Moribundus." All the doctors lowered their heads and walked solemnly out the door.

From that day on, the patient gained strength. In just a

few days he was much better. In fact, he got so much better that he went home from the hospital.

His doctors were amazed, and during a follow-up visit, someone asked him what had changed. He replied, "You told me that if a doctor could diagnosis my situation, I'd get well. That last doctor gave the diagnosis, whatever that word was."

The doctors didn't tell the patient, but do you know what *moribundus* means? It means dying. The patient didn't know that. He just understood it as a diagnosis, and his mind was stronger than the disease in his body. He overcame his illness.

Let me tell you, what you think is what will happen. If transformed people want to make the most of every day, we simply need to do it. Reflect it. Focus on the good and pure and true.

Dear Lord, I hear your diagnosis. Administer your medicine to me and create within me a cheerful heart. Strengthen my mind and body so that I may follow you to the ends of the earth.

23
The Game's Not Over

"And whoever compels you to go one mile, go with him two." (Matthew 5:41, NKJV)

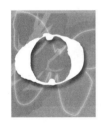ne Friday afternoon I saw a baseball game. Trinity and Alabama Christian were playing in the state semifinals. Trinity was behind six to one, going into the last inning. Everybody thought it was all over—except the Trinity baseball team.

With two outs and down five runs, nobody would have faulted the team for giving up. But they didn't give up. A rally started and the bases were loaded. A Trinity player was up at bat. With a swift, loud *whack*, he drove the ball in the gap between right and center field and cleaned the bases! Trinity scored six runs and won the game. The team never gave up.

In Jesus' day, the law said that a Roman soldier could, at any time, demand a civilian to carry his pack. These packs were filled with the soldier's clothes and all the utensils the soldier needed. They were very heavy. Jesus said if a Roman soldier asked you to carry his pack for a mile, you should say to him, "Good, may I also carry it an extra mile?" Just think, a good Jewish person could be dressed up for synagogue, going to work, or going out with the family, and all of a sudden, a soldier could stop the person and demand that he carry his pack. Civilians were required to stop whatever they were doing, pick up the pack, and walk for a mile.

The law said a civilian could set the pack down at exactly a mile, but Jesus said when you finish that mile, ask the soldier if you can carry it for another. You see, the second mile is the mile that means the most in life.

Do you know what happens in life so often? People give up right when victory is around the corner. Folks quit; they get disheartened and give up. But the mile that means the most is the mile when you go beyond what's expected. It's the mile of perseverance.

Father, give me the strength to go the extra mile today.

24
Scrap Iron

"Look, as the clay is in the potter's hand, so are you in My hand." (Jeremiah 18:6b, NKJV)

found a piece of scrap iron in a pile ready to be thrown away. But, you know, this piece of iron could be very valuable if it were made into something. Right now, it's just a piece of scrap iron. It's not worth very much. Really not worth anything. But, you know, if you took this piece of iron and melted it down and made it into horseshoes, it would be worth about $20. Or, if instead of horseshoes, you melted it down and made it into needles, it would be worth about $200. Or, if instead of needles, you took it and melted it down and some artisan made balance springs for watches, this piece of scrap iron could be worth about $200,000. It's not worth much like it is; it's going to be thrown away. But look at what it could become if the right person got hold of it.

Our lives are exactly like that. We're not worth very much. We are just like pieces of iron on a scrap heap. God takes our lives and transforms us. He makes us into something that's valuable and wonderful.

To every one of us, God gives a purpose.

Jeremiah is a great Old Testament character. One day God spoke to him and said, "Come on, Jeremiah. Walk with me down to the marketplace." At the marketplace, he watched a man making a pitcher out of clay. The man molded the pitcher, and then looked at it. He saw an imperfection, tore it up, and then reshaped the clay until was right.

God said to Jeremiah, "You want to know your purpose? You're like that clay. If you put your life in my hands, I'll make something out of it. What you've made is a mess. I'll tear it up, and redo it."

God has a plan for transformed people. He wants to take us into his hands and make us what we ought to be.

Father, my life has so many imperfections. Please take me into your hands and mold me, shape me, into something that is useful to you.

25
The Right Time

*So let's not allow ourselves to get fatigued doing good. At
the right time we will harvest a good crop if we don't give
up, or quit. Right now, therefore, every time we get the
chance, let us work for the benefit of all, starting with the
people closest to us in the community of faith. (Galatians
6:10, The Message)*

hen I finished seminary, I became the
associate minister and youth minister at
Capital Heights Methodist Church in
Montgomery, Alabama. One night we went
out to visit some of the young people in
Montgomery. A young man named Jim and I went to a boy's
house about seven o'clock, but the boy wasn't at home. We
went back at eight o'clock, and he wasn't at home. We went
back at nine o'clock, and for the third time, the boy was not
at home. I told Jim it was about time for us to go home, but
his response surprised me.

Jim said, "I thought we were going to visit Tom."

"We did, but he's not at home," I said.

"You know, I bet he'll come home sometime tonight. If we park in front of his house, we'll be there when he comes home."

So we sat outside Tom's house until he came home. And, you know what? We were the right people at the right place at the right time. God touched that young person's life that night.

Let me fast forward about fifteen years. I was privileged to place my hands on Tom's head as he was commissioned as a missionary to South America. What if Jim and I had gone home that night as I had suggested?

It's easy to get tired and go home and watch TV, but transformed people need to set aside our earthly desires and to listen to the Lord. When he says, "Keep at it; be persistent; don't give up," he means it.

Dear Heavenly Father, I praise your name. Your will is so beyond my understanding. Guide me along the path that you want me to walk. Introduce me to the people you want me to meet. I want to set aside my earthly desires and listen to you, Father.

26
Pray Expectantly

"Whatever you ask for in prayer with faith, you will receive." (Matthew 21:22, NRSV)

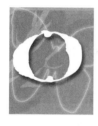ne day a man noticed his son tying a big rope to the back porch. He said, "Son, what are you doing that for?" The little boy responded, "Dad, you know I've been praying for God to bring me a pony. So, I want to give God something to tie the pony to when he brings him."

Jesus said in Matthew 7, "Ask and it will be given to you." Could that possibly be right? Just ask, and it's going to come my way? Jesus didn't say, "It might." He said, "It will."

If you pray for rain, carry an umbrella with you. Pray expectantly. There's never a prayer that goes unanswered. So, expect an answer. Now, the answer is not always what we want, but it's God's will. If I go to the grocery store, I expect to find food. If I go to the gas station, I expect to find gas. If I pick up the phone, I expect to hear a dial tone. You know what God said? "If you pray, expect me to respond to what you're asking for." Transformed people pray expectantly.

We read in Acts 12 that when Peter was in prison, a group of Christians decided to pray for Peter to be released from prison. God heard their prayer and sent an angel to set Peter free. When he was released, Peter went to the house where the believers were praying. The women heard a knock at the gate and sent a young girl by the name of Rhoda to see who was there. She was so shocked to see Peter that she turned and ran to tell the others, instead of letting Peter inside the gate and into the house. She ran back to the rest of the group and said, "You're not going to believe who's here!"

Tough times have a way of occupying every waking moment. Have you been so totally consumed with the issues that you didn't have time to pray, much less expect God to hear your prayers? If you want to use your time wisely, stop right now and pray. Pray expectantly.

Father, I praise your name. Thank you for answering my prayers. Help me to grow in your strength and to expect your will to be done.

27

Fear Versus Reality

"Do not fear, for I have redeemed you; I have called you by name, you are mine." (Isaiah 43:1b, NRSV)

 medical missionary was working in Africa when he started noticing many of the local people were dying. When he examined the people, he could find nothing wrong, but the people kept dying. Finally, someone told him that a witch doctor had placed a death curse on certain people. Those people had become so fearful of the curse that they died!

Fear will replace reality. When something happens, you can become so afraid that you don't see things clearly. Matthew 25 records a story Jesus told about a man who entrusted different sums of money to three of his workers. Two of the workers invested the money wisely, which resulted in even more money. But one of them said, "I was afraid, and I went and hid your talent in the ground" (verse

25). His fear paralyzed him and kept him from doing what was expected of him.

A little boy was going into surgery for an appendectomy. He was scared to death. When the orderly was rolling the bed out of the door, the little boy looked at me and said, "John Ed, I'll see you in heaven."

About twenty minutes later, the doctor came in the room and said, "I need to ask you a question. The orderly said that this little boy said, 'I'll see you in heaven.' Is that true?"

I said, "Yes, sir. He did say that."

The doctor replied, "We're not going to do the surgery today." He went on to explain that there are indications that if a person thinks he or she will die and then is put to sleep, there is a chance that the person might die. He said, "I want some people to talk to him and help him get over his fear."

Fear will lock a person down. Fear will kill you if you're not careful. But God says that faith can replace fear. We don't need to be locked down with fear. We can have faith.

Transformed people have not received the spirit of slavery leading to fear, but we have received the spirit of adoption as children. God didn't give us a spirit to be a slave to fear.

Heavenly Father, I am passing through the rivers of tough times. Be with me and keep the waters from sweeping over me. You are the Lord, my God.

28

Somebody Knows Where the Light Switch Is

The people living in darkness have seen a great light; on those living in the land of the shadow of death a light has dawned. (Matthew 4:16, NIV)

 little boy stood at the very bottom of the Carlsbad Caverns in New Mexico. He and his dad were part of a tour to the famous caverns. When the tour guide turned out the lights, the caverns became pitch dark and the little boy started to cry. The boy's daddy reached down, took boy's hand, and said, "Son, don't worry. There's somebody in here who knows where the light switch is."

When life looks the darkest, somebody, Almighty God our Father, knows where the light switch is. He'll turn on light at the proper time.

Luke wrote about a dark night when an angel appeared to some shepherds out in the field. Luke says these men were scared, but the first words the angel said were *fear not.*

Then again, Matthew wrote about Jesus' resurrection. He said when the women went to the tomb and saw that it was empty, they were scared. And what happened? An angel appeared to them and said, "Don't be afraid. Fear not."

If we allow it to, fear can replace reality. The little boy standing in the dark cavern was afraid; he felt like he was all alone. When he felt his daddy's hand and heard his daddy's voice, he feared not. He had faith that his daddy would make everything be all right.

Fear not; don't be afraid. This encouragement, this command, appears 365 times in the Bible. Now, that's once for every day of the year. Transformed people don't have to be afraid. Our Father God is with us, holding our hand, 365 days of the year. With God we have faith, and faith replaces fear.

Father God, I pray that you will turn on the light. Tough times have made my world so dark. I need your light, your strength. Hold my hand and turn on the light.

29

Little Ropes Tie Up Big People

An evil man is held captive by his own sins; they are ropes that catch and hold him. He will die for lack of self-control; he will be lost because of his great foolishness. (Proverbs 5:22-23, NLT)

 o you remember Jonathan Swift's story *Gulliver's Travels*? Six-foot-tall Gulliver was shipwrecked and washed up on the shore of Lilliput, an island where all the people were six inches tall. Those little bitty six-inch people tied up that big six-foot fellow with teeny-tiny little ropes. They wrapped enough rope around the man that he couldn't get up. I don't think I'll ever forget the first time I had that mental picture—I still have it today—this big, huge guy lying there with these little ropes tying him down.

One summer evening I returned home from a speaking engagement only to be greeted by a hot house! The air conditioner had gone out, and who knows how long it had been off. When the serviceman finally came out, he looked at me and smiled. He said, "You are not going to believe what's wrong with your air conditioner." He pointed to a little twig about an inch long that had fallen into the fan and jammed the fan blade against the casing of the air conditioner. That little bitty twig (now an expensive twig) got into the one place that would shut down all the cool air to the house.

How many times do we let little things get into our spiritual life and play havoc? We might think that because something is small, that it is insignificant. Little things in the wrong places can mess up an entire operation.

You know, I see real people all the time tied down that same way. Big people tied down by little things—a habit, a hang up, or a hurt. Sometimes it's a bad temper; a tendency to use profanity; overeating; addiction to alcohol, exercise, or work.

Satan loves, more than anything else, to take little ropes and wrap them around us until we can't move. He lures us into falling for his temptations, and let me tell you, if we fall to temptation, we're going to get tied up.

Transformed people can break free of those little ropes. If we hear and act on the truth, Jesus Christ, we will be set free. God's greatest desire is to see folks get free of those little ropes—to be released from earthly bonds—and follow Him.

Heavenly Father, thank you for your grace that sets me free of earthly ropes. Help me to stand on your Word and reflect your glory.

30
God's Economics

"A man's life does not consist in the abundance of his pos-
sessions." (Luke 12:15b, NIV)

n Matthew 25:14-30, Jesus told a story
about three men who were given bags of
money. A man was going on a journey and
called three of his servants to hold onto his
money for him. One man was given five
bags, the second man was given two bags, and the third man
was given one bag. When the man returned from his journey, he called the three servants and asked for his money
back.

The man with five bags said, "Look, I've got 10 bags of
money for you." The man with two bags said, "I've got four
bags of money for you." Now, the third man had been afraid
of losing his master's money. He dug a hole in the ground
and hid his bag, and on the day of accountability, he had the
one bag of money that the master had given him.

In 2008, the United States experienced an economic upheaval. Some of the country's largest businesses were in trouble. AIG, Lehman Brothers, Merrill-Lynch, Wachovia, and others had to admit that they had mismanaged the money that their customers had entrusted them. This major blunder was felt all over the world.

Obviously, human theories of economics are faulty. Most folks used to believe that the American economic system was a place where you could put your faith. However, that belief has been shaken by developments in the stock market and the economy. Even the strongest economic system in the world cannot be completely trusted. But God can be. His economics is not about accumulating things. It is about the quality of life that results from a relationship with God through Jesus Christ.

Transformed people are to invest in eternal things, not worldly things. Our CFO, the Lord Jesus Christ, calls the shots, and he doesn't make mistakes!

Dear Lord, I put my trust in you. Help me to make the right decisions today.

31
A False Sense of Security

"No one lights a lamp and puts it in a place where it will be hidden, or under a bowl. Instead he puts it on its stand, so that those who come in may see the light." (Luke 11:33, NIV)

hen things get out of focus, they are not what they appear to be. I heard about a young woman who went shopping and found a beautiful sweater. It was so pretty that she had to buy it. She brought the sweater home and put it in a trunk. She was going to save it for a special occasion. Days and years went by, and so did plenty of special occasions, but none were special enough to wear that beautiful sweater. Finally, the occasion came. It was a special event and the sweater was perfect for the occasion. The woman went to the trunk and pulled out her beautiful sweater, but it came out in strings. All the time she kept her beautiful sweater in a trunk and never wore it.

Now, let me tell you, the world is full of people with that

mentality. They think if they hide treasures away and don't use them, they won't lose them. Reality is just the opposite. You won't lose it if you do use it. If you put a patch over your eye for three months, do you know what will happen? You'll lose the sight in your eye. Put a cast on your arm for three months and your muscles will atrophy. When the cast comes off, you can't use the arm.

Two men were learning to speak Spanish. The first man went to class every day, studied, and turned in his homework on time, every time. The second man skipped a class or two and was a little late with his homework, but he aced the exam while the first man made a B- in the class. What made the difference? The first man never tried to speak the language; he simply did the classwork. The second man skipped class to work in the field with migrant workers. He used what little Spanish he had learned and even learned more by talking with the workers. He used what he was learning; he didn't save his knowledge for another day.

A lot of folks think, *if I can just get enough money, or enough fame, or enough recognition at work, and just hang on to it, I won't lose it.* The truth is, if you fall into the trap of that kind of thinking, you will end up one day with nothing. Jesus said, "If you want to have it, then give it away."

Lord, you give me so much. Show me how you want me to use your wonderful gifts.

32
Traversing Mountains

"Blessed are those who trust in the Lord, whose trust is the Lord. They shall be like a tree planted by water, sending out its roots by the stream. It shall not fear when heat comes, and its leaves shall stay green; in the year of drought it is not anxious, and it does not cease to bear fruit." (Jeremiah 17:7-8, NRSV)

arcus Whitman was a man of vision. According to an old story, he traveled the Oregon Trail and set up a mission in Oregon. At the time, the Oregon territory could have been claimed by either Great Britain or the United States. Some American politicians were ready to give up the territory because they thought the mountains were impassable; settling Oregon would be very difficult.

But Whitman went back East and tried to get more families to move out West, convinced that if he could make the trip, others could too. In Washington, DC, he met with several senators and representatives who thought the task was impossible. So Whitman went to President Tyler to try to encourage people to move West. Tyler was a skeptic too. He said that men on horseback could cross the mountains, but wagons and families just couldn't make it.

But Whitman persevered, arguing for Oregon's importance to the future of the country and for his belief that immigration was possible. He eventually persuaded President Tyler, who assured him the immigrants would receive the protection of the United States.

When tough times come around, lots of people are ready to tell you that you can't make it. You'll have to give up. The mountains are too rugged for a mere person to conquer. And, honestly, that's true. A mere person can't traverse rugged mountains, but transformed people are not traveling alone. We are following God. Don't ever let a mere person tell you that something can't be done. If God wants it done, even the roughest mountains will be conquered.

Heavenly Father, my confidence is in you. My conviction is unswerving. Your glorious will, will be done.

33
Running With Weights

Let us throw off everything that hinders and the sin that so easily entangles, and let us run with perseverance the race marked out for us. (Hebrews 12:1b, NIV)

he biggest athletic event in New Testament times was "the human race." The Olympics developed from these competitions. History shows that runners in training for these races put huge weights on their ankles and practiced running with the weights. This built up endurance and strengthened their muscles and lungs. When it came time for the race, the runners would take off the weights. A person who tried to run in a competition with weights around their ankles would certainly get tripped up and bogged down.

Athletes still use weights like this today. If you put weights around your ankles, you would see that it is a little hard to walk, but when used cautiously, they are a great training aid. Now, I wouldn't dare try to go down steps with weights on my ankles. They would trip me up. And, if I'm going to go out and really do some walking, I don't want to wear ankle weights.

You know, when a person has been wearing these weights for a while and then takes them off, they not only function better, but they can walk a lot easier too. Now it's important when you take them off that you don't keep them in your hand and walk around with them all day. It's one thing to take them off the ankles, but it's another thing to take them off completely.

During tough times, every one of us has some sort of weights that we are walking around with. We either have them around our ankles or are carrying them in our hand. But transformed people can take off those weights, put them down completely. If you are going to follow God, and you've still got these weights on, you're going to get tripped up and you won't be able to go very far.

Heavenly Father, help me take the weights off of my ankles and remove them completely so that I can follow you without stumbling. I want to run and not faint.

34
Listen Closely

While he was still speaking, a bright cloud enveloped them, and a voice from the cloud said, "This is my Son, whom I love; with him I am well pleased. Listen to him!" (Matthew 17:5, NIV)

ears ago, before the invention of refrigerators, some families had an icebox in their house. This was during a time when money was scarce, so some communities would have a little icehouse where people could bring their vegetables and meats. Someone was in charge of putting ice in the little house and covering it with straw to keep it from melting so quickly.

One day about a dozen men were working at an icehouse. It was nearly full with lots of food and a lot of ice. Late in the afternoon one of the men realized his watch had fallen off while he was working. The men all stopped what they were doing and helped look for the watch. They spent about forty-five minutes searching through the food, ice, and straw, but they couldn't find it.

When they stepped outside to take a break, a ten-year-old boy walked into the icehouse. In about thirty seconds he walked out and said, "Does this watch belong to anybody?"

The men gathered around the boy and said, "How did you find it? We looked for forty-five minutes and couldn't find it."

The boy replied, "Oh, it wasn't hard. I just went in, got real quiet, and put my ear up to the straw. When I heard the watch ticking, I just reached in and pulled it out of the straw."

We, as transformed people, need to get real quiet, put our ear up to the heart of God, and listen to what he is trying to tell us.

Heavenly Father, open my ears that I might hear your voice today. I need you to guide me through the tough times that face me today.

35
Stash the Gnash

The LORD is compassionate and gracious, slow to anger abounding in love. He will not always accuse, nor will he harbor his anger forever; he does not treat us as our sins deserve or repay us according to our iniquities. For as high as the heavens are above the earth, so great is his love for those who fear him; as far as the east is from the west, so far has he removed our transgressions from us. (Psalm 103:8-12, NIV)

ow do you react when you face tough times? Are you grumpy? Do you spew angry words? Do you glare at people nearest you? Well, let me tell you a little story about a man named Otto Graham.

He was quarterback for the Cleveland Browns when they played the Rams for the championship in 1950. The Browns were behind by one point and moving down the field in the final two minutes. They only needed a field goal to win. Graham ran a quarterback draw and picked up about ten yards, but he fumbled the ball, which was recovered by the Rams. Graham later said he had never felt so downhearted. He thought he had blown their chance to win.

As he came off the field, he saw Coach Paul Brown coming toward him. Graham's stomach tightened. He was ready for a reprimand, but Brown reassured him, saying they would still find a way to win the game.

That little bit of encouragement boosted Graham's emotions so much that the team went on to win 30 to 28!

Graham recalled that Paul Brown knew when to kick you in the pants and when to pat you on the shoulder. He said that if the coach had glared at him at that moment, the Browns would have lost. Instead his encouragement gave Graham and the rest of the team the confidence to go back down the field and score the three points they needed.

When we face tough times, it's hard not to feel downhearted, to glare at or scold those nearest to us. But, everyone responds better to encouragement than an angry scolding. Everybody will make mistakes. A little encouragement might turn a "fumble" into a "winning score."

Heavenly Father, cool my temper and give me the words to encourage rather than discourage. Thank you, Father, for standing beside me through these tough times.

36
The Power of Living Water

Now to him who by the power at work within us is able to accomplish abundantly far more than all we can ask or imagine, to him be glory in the church and in Christ Jesus to all generations, forever and ever. Amen. (Ephesians 3:20-21, NRSV)

 uring the hot summers in Montgomery, Alabama, we always have a little shortage of rain. Everyone talks about the dams that supply our electricity and whether there will be enough water to keep our air conditioners and laptop computers going. One time somebody asked a man who was operating one of the big dams that generate power, "How much of the power of the water can you harness?" He said, "Only a very small amount—about one one-hundredth of the total power available."

Imagine the power of flowing water. Technology has enabled man to harness one one-hundredth of the power of flowing water and create enough electricity to power thousands of homes and businesses. Now, how much more powerful is the Living Water of God? We can't possibly imagine the enormity of God's power. How much of God's power are we using for our lives? God's power supply is greater than any of us can ever use, but are we running at maximum strength?

God's power is unending. He will give us as much power as we need to accomplish the tasks he places before us. Look at Luke 10. Jesus sent seventy-two workers to precede him in other towns. He gave them power to heal the sick, trample on snakes and scorpions, and to overcome all the power of the enemy. But it was only because they were filled with the power of the Holy Spirit that they could do these things. They were filled with the power in order to pave the way for Jesus.

The most powerful thing in the world is the power of the Holy Spirit. It is only because of God's holy power flowing through us that we can carry out his commands and pave the way for him.

Dear Lord, without your power, I cannot move. I want to walk in obedience to you. Fill me with your power so that I may pave the way for you.

37
Telling Time

Everything on earth has its own time and its own sea-son. . . . God makes everything happen at the right time. (Ecclesiastes 3:1, 11a, CEV)

ave you seen the watch with the hands that run backward? With this watch, you'll never get behind. You can also get watches with jumbled figures and upside down designs. If you are really confused about how to use your time, one of these watches might be helpful.

A clockmaker has created a way to give us a little more time. He has invented a clock that operates on a 57.6-second minute. By shaving 2.4 seconds off each minute, you end up with an extra hour at the end of the day.

All these man-made contraptions are just a trick. We all have the same amount of time each day, and we need to use it effectively.

The Bible has the best solution for time management. If

we seek first God's kingdom (Matthew 6:33) then other things will fall into their proper place. Keeping correct time is not nearly as important as using our time as good stewards. We need to be able to tell time, but how we use our time is more important.

Managing our time is not always easy, especially during tough times. We get bogged down in our activities and allow the small details to throw our schedule behind. Then the more we get behind, the more anxious we become. Philippians 4:6-7 says it all—when we give our anxiety over to the Lord, we will be filled with his peace and calm. All we need to do is present our requests to God, and he will comfort our hearts and minds.

Oh, Lord, I need time management today. Please fill my soul with your perfect timing and direct my actions today.

38
God's Way

"It is not for you to know the times or the seasons, which the Father hath put in his own power." (Acts 1:7, KJV)

riday, February 12, 2010, was the first time in recorded history that every state in the United States had snow on the ground on the same day. There was some question about Hawaii, but I understand that there was snow on some of the mountain ranges. There was snow in Florida and all the southeastern states.

That was also the weekend that the Winter Olympics began in Vancouver, one place in North America where there was a lack of snow! Olympic organizers spent millions of dollars to haul snow in to the slopes so they could have enough snow for the downhill ski runs. But the temperature was so warm that the snow didn't last! Those green ski slopes were some sight.

You know, God is God. The more we try to figure out the

way he is going to do things, the more surprises he has for us. We can plan our lives out perfectly, but then God has an entirely different idea.

Years ago there was a popular bumper sticker that said "God is my co-pilot." But, you know what? God is not our co-pilot; he is our pilot! He is in total charge and can accomplish things without our help at all. We, as transformed people, are privileged to have God invite us to participate in the fulfillment of his plan.

God's thoughts are not like our thoughts, according to Isaiah: "Just as the heavens are higher than the earth so are . . . my thoughts higher than your thoughts" (Isaiah 55:9, NCV). I think some things are so logical, then God shows me how human logic does not compare to his logic. God sees things from a totally different perspective.

Thank you, Lord, for the snow. Thank you for reminding me that the best laid human plans are totally irrelevant when your plan comes into place. Help me remember that your way is the best way, and my responsibility is to be obedient to your plan.

39
Down—But Not Out

I can do everything through him who gives me strength.
(Philippians 4:13, NIV)

 t was the greatest game in NFL history! It occurred in 1993. I watched it and had a hard time believing it. At halftime Houston was ahead 28 to 3. The announcers had already given the game to Houston and were interviewing the coach of the Pittsburgh Steelers, asking him how he would play Houston in the next round of the playoffs.

Frank Reich, quarterback for the Buffalo Bills, had a different idea. Back in 1984 he had brought the University of Maryland back from a 31-point deficit against Miami. That also was a collegiate record.

Reich's pinpoint passing and perfect play calling in the second half engineered the comeback. Buffalo scored thirty-eight more points to win over Houston! (The final score was 41 to 38.) In the postgame interview, the first thing Reich said was that he gave the credit to Jesus who was most important in his life.

Later in the locker room interview he said the music to the Christian song "Christ Alone," by Michael English, was what gave him the composure and determination to win. He read the lyrics at the press conference. The heart of the song reads, "Though I can pride myself in battles won . . . by His strength alone I overcome."

Marv Levy, the coach of the Buffalo Bills, said he was surprised, but he had faith in Reich. He highly complimented his Christian faith. He said, "It is his faith that gives him so much composure and causes people to believe in him." Coach Levy said he would never count Buffalo out of any game as long as he had a man with the faith of Reich as quarterback.

The greatest strength in the world comes in our relationship with Jesus Christ. You are never out in any situation when you trust in him. Sometimes some situations seem hopeless, but "by His strength alone, I overcome." You may be down, but in Christ you're never out!

Heavenly Father, I know the score. Tough times have put me behind, but you are my Head Coach. I rely on you for all my strength.

40

Calling the Shots

By your words I can see where I'm going; they throw a beam of light on my dark path. (Psalm 119:105, The Message)

 atching football games on television grows more and more popular each year. The 2010 Super Bowl drew more viewers than any other program in the history of television. It's fun to go to a game, but you can see more when you watch it on TV. You get to see different camera angles and the replays.

The *Wall Street Journal* conducted a study and found that in a three-hour-plus televised football game, just over 11 minutes are actual playing time. The rest of the time is devoted to players going to the huddle, lining up for the play, crowd shots, coaches' antics, cheerleaders, and so forth. That means that the television game director calls the shots; he or she decides what we see the other 2 hours and 49 minutes. The game director uses many cameras and camera angles to be sure that the audience sees the play, plus aspects of the play that someone in the stands might not see. A good game director presents interesting aspects of the game.

When we are facing tough times, it's hard to figure out who is calling the shots in our game of life, but transformed people can rest assured that God is our Game Director. He views every part of our lives, and he is in charge. We don't have to rely on ourselves to make the right decisions. All we need to do is call on God and follow his guidance. He will determine how the game is presented. If we try to select the camera shots for our life, it would be a demonstration of sin—selfish exploitation. On the other hand, we can't let other people decide for us. They cannot see the whole playing field, and their perception will not be completely accurate.

God is our game director. He calls the shots. He gets the camera angles that tell who we really are. The "11 minutes" of our lives will have a tremendous impact when God is in control.

Dear Lord, you are the light that shines on my path. When tough times try to throw me off track, I focus my sight on you. Today, and every day, I concentrate on you, O Lord.

41
Life's Logjams

Cast your cares on the Lord and he will sustain you; he will
never let the righteous fall. (Psalm 55:22, NIV)

ave you ever watched a logging operation
near a river? The loggers move the cut logs
into the river, and the river carries them
down to the processing mill. Most of the
time, the logs will travel just so far, then get
tangled up into a "logjam." The logs start crossing over each
other, and before you know it, they can't move at all. The
loggers have to take long poles, separate the logs, and break
the logjam.

A group of doctors did a study and discovered four basic
things that make people vulnerable to disease. They are:
holding resentments; self-pity; difficulty in developing and
maintaining long-term relationships; and poor self-image.
Oftentimes, these emotions and tendencies form a logjam
in a person's life, and that's when the tough times really

begin. Just one or two of these can block a person's way and make him or her vulnerable not only to spiritual but also to physical and emotional disease.

I went into the church early one morning and discovered that the air-conditioner was not working. After talking with Rusty, the church administrator, I said, "Well, let's call the folks who can fix it, and get them out here." Rusty said, "No. I've learned how to start it." We walked outside to the unit, and Rusty picked up a stick. He whacked the unit with the stick, and suddenly the unit started. He said, "I'm not an engineer, but I know where to hit it."

Transformed people know what it's like to get a whack from God. I don't mean God picks up a stick and beats us. I mean he knows where to put his finger to separate the log-jam that tough times have caused. If we're willing to put forth the effort, God will separate the logjam of emotions in our heart. He will set us on a smooth, straight pathway.

Father, thank you for keeping my pathway straight. Help me avoid the logjams that come my way today.

42
Nothing Is Impossible

So we fix our eyes not on what is seen, but on what is unseen. For what is seen is temporary, but what is unseen is eternal. (2 Corinthians 4:18, NIV)

here's an interesting book on display in Washington, DC. It was written years ago in England by a mathematician. He used mathematical formulas to calculate the impossibility of a steamship ever crossing the Atlantic Ocean. Inside the front cover, someone inscribed, "This book was brought to America by the first steamship that crossed the Atlantic."

The world tells us that many things are impossible, and that we are not capable of completing the tasks God asks us to do. According to the world, even working on a relationship with God isn't worth the effort.

Do you know the Ohio state motto? It is "With God, all things are possible." Two young men who lived in Dayton proved this motto when they became the first men to fly an airplane. Orville and Wilbur Wright studied birds—what enabled them to take off, fly, and remain in the sky—and came up with a working design for human flight. They overcame the earthly wisdom that human flight was impossible, and used God's creations for their inspiration.

Early in the last century, a biologist and an aerodynamics expert were talking about how big old fat bumblebees with little bitty wings can fly. After doing a few calculations, the aerodynamicist decided that bumblebees didn't generate enough lift to fly. Now, he was comparing the bumblebee with an airplane. With further study, throughout the years, researchers say that bumblebees are more like helicopters than airplanes. Apparently, according to current theory anyway, a bee's wing muscles vibrate up and down like a guitar string. However, even though it looks impossible to humans, the little creatures are able to fly because God enables each and every one of them to glide through the sky and traverse our gardens every summer.

There are so many things that, in the human way of thinking, are impossible. However, God has no boundaries.

Dear Lord, I know that through you all things are possible. Thank you for the glorious blessings that you have given to me.

43
Making Excuses

No temptation has seized you except what is common to man. And God is faithful; he will not let you be tempted beyond what you can bear. But when you are tempted, he will also provide a way out so that you can stand up under it. (1 Corinthians 10:13, NIV)

 hen times get tough, it seems that making excuses for our mistakes is the appropriate thing to do. Many people believe the line that says, "It is easier to ask forgiveness than it is to ask for permission."

Really, that is a cheap view of forgiveness. It suggests that you can keep on doing the same thing over and over and always ask for forgiveness. Repentance in the Bible means that we ask for forgiveness with no intent of committing that sin again.

A man broke into the Berean Baptist Church in Ellenwood, Georgia. He took a lot of expensive equipment, including microphones and laptop computers containing important church records. He even broke the lock to the safe, but it was empty. But, that's not all—the robber scrawled a note on the wall saying, "I'm sorry, but I'm poor. Forgive me, Lord."

This was the fourth time the Berean Baptist Church had been robbed in two years. The pastor joked that he was going to post a sign telling robbers to call him before breaking in, and the church would take up a collection for them.

All too often, people choose to excuse their actions with a fainthearted request for forgiveness. That cheap concept of forgiveness is really just an excuse for sin.

The Bible is clear that each of us has sinned, but God desires to forgive us for our sins if we truly repent and confess. Confession is not a subtle excuse for our actions. It is the key to a right relationship with God and with other people. The Bible says that if we confess our sins, God is "faithful and just to forgive our sins, and to cleanse us from all unrighteousness" (1 John 1:9, KJV).

Father, I thank you for leading me through these tough times. Please forgive me for the sins that I have committed, and steer me away from fainthearted excuses.

44

Transformed People Are Never Alone

"Don't be afraid, for I am with you. Don't be discouraged, for I am your God. I will strengthen you and help you. I will hold you up with my victorious right hand." (Isaiah 41:10, NLT)

emptations are always strongest when we are in the middle of tough times. When our present looks bleak, Satan tries to tell us the future is going to be bleaker. He makes us feel alone in the midst of a crowd of people. He can make us feel distanced from the people who care for us and from the circumstances that we must face.

We do not have to struggle alone. God is always with us, in good times and in tough times. We are so precious to him that he has promised to be with us, no matter what we go through. Actually, one of the many names used for Jesus is Immanuel, which means, "God is with us." Long before Jesus' birth, the prophet Isaiah declared that a "virgin will conceive a child! She will give birth to a son and will call him Immanuel (which means 'God is with us')" (Isaiah 7:14, NLT). This verse from Isaiah is repeated in Matthew 1:23.

Jesus himself reassured us in Matthew 28:20, "Be sure of this: I am with you always, even to the end of the age" (NLT). When Jesus told the disciples, beginning in John 14, that he was leaving them, he told them to rest assured that God would give them another Comforter, the Holy Ghost. And this Comforter will be with us always (verse 16).

Transformed people serve an ever-faithful God who will never abandon us, never leave us alone. Even and especially at times when we cannot seem to feel God's presence, God holds us tightly in his hands. When times are hard, God calls us to cling even more closely to him, our only source of life, strength, and hope.

Dear Lord, the days are so dark now. How can I find your light? Please comfort me and guide me out of the darkness of these troubled times.

45

Reaching Out to Others

Praise be to the God and Father of our Lord Jesus Christ,
the Father of compassion and the God of all comfort, who
comforts us in all our troubles, so that we can comfort those
in any trouble with the comfort we ourselves have received
from God. (2 Corinthians 1:3-4, NIV)

A friend tells a story about someone who did a nice thing for him when he was a kid. It had such an impact that he remembers it clearly even now.

When John was about eleven, he went to the hospital to have his appendix removed. In those days, when you had that done, you stayed in the hospital for a whole week with no TV, video games, or anything. You can imagine how awful an experience that would have been for an eleven-year-old.

The hospital didn't allow kids John's age to visit patients. However, one of John's friends snuck into the hospital anyway. The boy brought an entire backpack of games, and the two boys played all day.

Remembering the day, John said, "I don't even know what kind of trouble he got in. But I know he wanted to be with me that day. That meant a ton to me." Even at eleven, the boy understood that reaching out in friendship is worth the risk. He moved out of his comfort zone and risked getting caught to comfort a friend.

As transformed people, we need to surround ourselves with other Christians and remind each other that—tough times and good times—we're all in this together. We are more willing to step out and take risks when we know that we're not alone. Teaming with other Christians gives us moral support, keeps us on target when we get frustrated, and encourages us to go for it even during tough times.

Do you risk venturing outside your own comfort zone? Do you have a friend who needs comforting? Transformed people take risks when necessary to reach out and share God's love.

Heavenly Father, walk with me today. Guide me through the risks that I must take today. Stand beside me and hold my hand when it is time for me to step out of my comfort zone.

46
The Whole Picture

"Do not fear, only believe." (Mark 5:36b, NRSV)

 little boy not long ago jumped out of a tree house. He landed straight down on a piece of wood. And of course, there was a nail in the wood. The nail came right up through the boy's shoe. The boy saw the end of the nail sticking straight up, high above the top of his shoe, and began screaming. He screamed so loud that his mother ran out of the back door and immediately put him in the car and rushed him to the emergency room.

Do you know what happened when they got to the emergency room? The doctor took the boy's shoe off and the nail had gone right between the boy's toes. It didn't touch his foot at all, but the boy screamed and cried all the way to the hospital. All he could see was that nail coming up out of his shoe. He later told his mother that he had thought that he was going to have to have his foot amputated.

That happens in life so much. We get so upset because we see the nail up through the shoe, and we can't calm down long enough to understand the whole picture.

Take a look at the story of Shadrach, Meshach, and Abednego in the Book of Daniel. King Nebuchadnezzar built a big statue of himself and demanded that everyone bow to the statue. But the three friends Daniel tells us about refused to bow down before this idol. The men were punished by being thrown into a hot furnace. As Nebuchadnezzar watched the men in the fiery furnace, he said, "I thought we put three men in the furnace; now there are four!" When the men were called out of the furnace, everyone could see that they had not even been touched by the flames.

Now, our earthly way of thinking would have us believe the men could not help but be burned to ash, but when God is involved, we need to wait and see the whole picture. You see, God was with them in the furnace, so indeed there were four men as the king thought. And, God kept his servants from harm.

God, you are so good to me. Thank you for making a plan just for me. Help me to see the whole picture and not panic.

47
God's Collateral

"Fear not, for I have redeemed you; I have summoned you by name; you are mine. When you pass through the waters, I will be with you; and when you pass through the rivers, they will not sweep over you. When you walk through the fire, you will not be burned; the flames will not set you ablaze. For I am the LORD, your God, the Holy One of Israel, your Savior." (Isaiah 43:1b-3a, NIV)

 wealthy man in South Georgia gave about three million dollars to a Christian school. He had a passion to see young people educated and come to know Christ. Then one day the economy went sour and the man lost all of his money. Some of his friends—acquaintances— said, "I bet you're sad, aren't you? You gave away $3,000,000 and now you don't have anything. I bet you wish you had that money back, don't you?"

One of the important ingredients in economics is an

understanding of collateral. The world has one view; God's economics offers quite a different perspective.

The man said, "No, you don't understand. Everything I tried to hang on to I've lost. The only thing I really have is what I've given away."

Early in the twenty-first century, the world's economics got into trouble because collateral was taken lightly. We saw what happened when money was lent to people who did not have proper collateral. Subprime loans, mortgage lending, and questionable financing helped cause the bottom to drop out of the United States' economy and affected many other nations throughout the world.

God's economics teaches us that with God you don't have to put up any physical possessions as collateral. All God requires is for us to trust in him and commit to "do as I say." In God's economics, collateral is commitment with integrity. It is obedience. It is not just talking, but walking.

Heavenly Father, I rely on you. Guide me through today and show me how I can use my collateral to further your will.

48
The Wings of Eagles

Those who hope in the LORD will renew their strength. They will soar on wings like eagles; they will run and not grow weary, they will walk and not be faint. (Isaiah 40:31, NIV)

he Bible doesn't teach that Christians are to be exempt from tough times. However, transformed people are able to face tough times with a power that is not available to people who do not know God.

The prophet Isaiah points out that humans get tired, but God does not. Even young people stumble and fall. When tough times wear us down, God is ready to fill us with his strength and power.

When I learned how to play tennis, my first lesson was on how to serve. I was told that it was the most important thing I'd learn, too. When I went on to college, I practiced my serve three hundred times a day because, as any tennis player will tell you, serving is an advantage.

I had a Sunday school teacher who said the same thing about serving in life. "I don't care what you accomplish in life," that teacher said. "You'll never find happiness unless you lose your life in service." And God backs up that teacher. If we want life and all its fullness, the Bible tells us, it only comes when we lose ourselves in serving God. Tough times or not, we are to serve the Lord—and his children—with gladness.

Eagles are the only birds that can lock their wings and wait for the right wind. They wait for an updraft and never flap their wings. They just soar. God helps transformed people use even the tough times to build up and not tear down—to advance the fulfillment of his will. We can wait upon him, and when the time is right, we can use our wings like eagles and soar.

Transformed people are able to rejoice and serve others in the midst of troubled times because we have heaven's view. We can look beyond the earthly view and straight into the glories of heaven.

Heavenly Father, I want to stretch my wings and soar with the power you give me. Lead me through these troubled times and help me make the best use of my time in serving you and your children.

49
Pick Your Ruts

Let your eyes look straight ahead, fix your gaze directly before you. Make level paths for your feet and take only ways that are firm. Do not swerve to the right or the left; keep your foot from evil. (Proverbs 4:25-27, NIV)

ears ago, there was a well-traveled road called the Alcan Highway that stretched from Canada to Alaska. I've heard that before the road was paved, a big sign alongside it said, "Pick your ruts carefully. You're going to be in them for a long time." Whether our life consists of dirt roads or paved ones, it is like that Alcan Highway. There are a lot of lanes and ruts to choose from, and you'd better pick which one you want, because let me tell you, every one of them goes somewhere.

Some folks choose the fast lane. They want to cram a lot into life. Remember the story in Luke 15 about a young boy who wanted to get in the fast lane? He told his daddy things on the farm were too dull. He wanted to go to the city and live it up. The Bible says he threw away his money on women, wine, and partying. This guy was living it up. Then he couldn't find work, and he ran out of money. You see the fast lane can slow down real quickly. Sometimes it ends. You've seen those signs on the interstate "Merge right. Lane ends." That boy's lane ran out. He was hungry and the only job he could find was feeding pigs. He made an interesting discovery: the fast lane usually ends up in a pigpen.

A lot of folks today choose that fast lane. They want more and more and more. They try to cram about thirty-six hours into every twenty-four-hour day. They get so involved doing so many things so quickly, that they miss the sign that says, "Merge right. Tough times ahead." Folks who choose that fast lane need to watch out, or they will wind up in a pigpen.

Heavenly Father, I praise your name. Thank you for guiding me into the right lane. Help me make the most of the road that I am traveling.

50
God Fulfills Our Needs

My God will meet all your needs according to his glorious riches in Christ Jesus. (Philippians 4:19, NIV)

od always provided Elijah with what he needed. First Kings 17 includes three examples. During those days, there was a drought and not enough food to eat. Surely Elijah wondered what was going to happen to him. God said to him, "Go down and sit by the brook, and every morning and evening I'll send ravens who will bring you bread and meat." And Elijah was fed. He had faith that God would meet his needs.

Elijah then went to a town and saw a woman gathering sticks outside the town's gate. He said to her, "Give me something to eat." And, she said, "Sir, we don't have anything to eat. All I have is one small jug of oil and a jar of meal. I'm going home, and I'm going to make some bread. My son and I are going to sit down and eat that bread, and then we're going to die because there is no other food." Elijah told her not to worry, that God was going to provide. He said, "You make enough for me also, and we'll all eat." And, you know what? She kept making bread, and that jar of meal and jug of oil were never exhausted. They never ran out. Elijah had faith, and God provided totally.

Sometime later, that woman's son became ill to the point that he was not breathing. Elijah prayed; God intervened; and the child was revived. In every incident of history, when Elijah faced difficulty, he discovered that God would provide what is necessary.

Faith helps transformed people get through tough times as well as good times. When we focus on our faith in the midst of our present circumstances, God provides us with everything that we need.

Father, thank you for providing for me in good times and tough times. Allow me to tell the world about your generosity and love.

51
Prayer Is Powerful

Be joyful always; pray continually; give thanks in all cir-
cumstances, for this is God's will for you in Christ Jesus.
(1 Thessalonians 5:16-17, NIV)

n the early part of 2010, a fifty-seat regional
aircraft took off from LaGuardia airport,
only to make an emergency landing
twenty-five minutes into the flight. A sev-
enteen-year-old passenger wearing a white
sweater took out something that he had carried onboard
and strapped it onto his arm and his head. Someone on the
flight crew noticed this unusual behavior and reported it to
the pilot, who immediately landed the plane.

The flight crew and some of the passengers were unfa-
miliar with the Jewish practice that is a part of the morning
prayer. Tefillin are small leather boxes attached to leather
straps that observant Jews wear during prayer. After being
checked out at the Philadelphia airport, the young man was

cleared of any wrongdoing and the plane resumed its flight to Kentucky.

Not everybody prays the same way. And, some don't pray at all. There is a lot of debate about whether we should pray in public, in private, kneeling, standing, and so forth. We ought to learn more about the way other people pray. It might inform us and educate us. It also might keep us from being as judgmental or developing a tendency to stereotype people because they might pray differently from the way we pray.

The young man's rabbi gave him advice for future flights. He said, "I would suggest, pray on the plane and put the tefillin on later. Pray now and fulfill the ritual later."

Prayer is powerful. The mere fact that a young man was praying caused a plane and all of its passengers to change plans immediately. Prayer can redirect and give people a different ultimate destination.

Dear Lord, thank you for teaching your children to pray. Help me to honor your name. Give me what I need for today, and forgive my sins as I forgive those who have done wrong to me.

52

Caught Up in
the Unimportant

*"For I know the plans I have for you," says the LORD. "They
are plans for good and not for disaster, to give you a future
and a hope." (Jeremiah 29:11, NLT)*

ough times have a way of drawing our
focus to the situation at hand. How are we
going to pay the bills this week? What can
we say to comfort our daughter? Each of
the questions that develops because of
tough times has a way of casting a shadow on our emotions
and attitudes.

A teenage boy had some miserable older brothers. They
were so jealous of the boy that they sold him into slavery.
The boy eventually ended up in prison, but after several
years, he caught the attention of the king of Egypt. The king
was so impressed with the young man that he placed him in
the highest position in the land, second only to the king
himself. Since he was in charge of Egypt, he saved years'

worth of abundant harvest and was able to use it in the time of famine.

You know by now that this is the story of Joseph. Read the whole story beginning in Genesis 37.

Joseph went through some tough times, but God used each of those difficult events as stepping-stones in his plan for saving people from famine. In the course of the events, Joseph was reunited with his brothers, and he was able to tell them, "You intended to harm me, but God intended it for good to accomplish what is now being done, the saving of many lives" (Genesis 50:20, NIV).

Transformed people don't need to live in the shadow of tough times. We can rest assured that God is in control each step of the way. He has a plan for our lives, and that plan is for good, not disaster. We don't know what the future holds, and we don't need to fret about it. We only need to focus on God, our hope.

Father, thank you for loving me so much that you have my future planned. Thank you for resolving my questions and allowing me time to focus on you.

53
Doing the Best We Can

"I call to the Lord, who is worthy of praise, and I am saved from my enemies." (2 Samuel 22:4, NIV)

 hen we face a tough situation, we have two choices: we can see the situation as a problem or as a possibility. The earthly attitude focuses on problems. The Christlike attitude focuses on possibilities.

A story goes that during World War II, a group of French soldiers was captured by the Germans and made to work in a German munitions factory, making bombs. They knew that some of those bombs would be dropped on their own people, possibly even their own families. Now, these guys were certainly facing some tough times.

As time went by, one of the captives, a scientist, turned the problem into a possibility. He figured out a way to construct the bombs so that they wouldn't actually detonate when they hit. He taught the other soldiers to make them that way too.

When the bombing started in France, those bombs went down, but sure enough, they wouldn't explode. Experts were called in to find out what was going on, and when they disassembled one of the nondetonating bombs, they found a note inside. It said something like, "Doing the best we can, with what we have, where we are."

I have discovered that attitude is more important than the reality of situations. I've seen people who were facing similar situations emerge with opposite results because of their attitudes. We have little or no control over the situation itself, but we can and must be in control of our attitude. In my opinion, attitude determines the outcome of most situations.

Paul reminds us in Philippians 2:5, "Your attitude should be the same as that of Christ Jesus" (NIV). The attitude that will help us transcend tough times is the attitude that Jesus had.

Father, thank you for sending your Son to be a role model for me. Guide me through these tough times as I try to develop a Christlike attitude.

54
Helping Each Other

Let us think of ways to motivate one another to acts of love and good works. (Hebrews 10:24, NLT)

hen was the last time you played volleyball? You remember; there are two teams of six players on opposite sides of a net. The server on each team is on the back row, and the spikers are on the front row. The object of the game is to get the ball over the net and not have it returned by the opposing team.

Now, who is the most important person on the team? Is it the server? The spikers? What about the other folks on the team in other positions? Are they on the team just to sit back and earn the glory of winning? No. Everyone on the team plays an important part. They each support the others and work toward a common goal.

Think about the winning teams you've seen in the past. One of the things those teams have in common is that they're passionate about reaching their goals—dunking that basket, making that touchdown, or hitting that home run. And they're passionate about doing it together. These are the folks who understand that old saying that there's no "I" in "team."

If we, as members of God's team, are going to be successful in these tough times, we need to pick up a few habits from those winning sports teams. We don't have to learn any end zone dances, but we do need to give our all for the common good. We need to serve our brothers and sisters when they are facing tough times, and in turn serve God.

Winning teams—in volleyball or in any other sport—are set apart because they're willing to help one another. The individual members are willing to step back and let someone else with greater skills and abilities step forward to accomplish the task.

We must encourage and support one another, especially during tough times. Teaming with other Christians gives us moral support, keeps us on target when we get frustrated, and encourages us to go for it even during tough times. In Galatians 6:2, Paul says, "Share each other's burdens, and in this way obey the law of Christ" (NLT).

Dear Lord, thank you for making me a part of your winning team. Remind me to help others as they help me.

55
Affecting the Future

It is impossible for those who have once been enlightened, who have tasted the heavenly gift, who have shared in the Holy Spirit, who have tasted the goodness of the word of God and the powers of the coming age, if they fall away, to be brought back to repentance, because to their loss they are crucifying the Son of God all over again and subjecting him to public disgrace. (Hebrews 6:4-6, NIV)

 ezekiah became king when he was twenty-five years old. And what a king he was! In 2 Kings 18, we learn that he was a godly man, always faithful to the Lord. Judah never had another ruler like him, either before or after his time. He looked to the Lord for everything, and he was successful in everything he did.

When Hezekiah became ill and was about to die, he wasn't ready to go. He wept and prayed. God heard his prayers and gave him another fifteen years to live. During that time, however, Hezekiah became proud and selfish. He began to trust in his own strength, rather than God's.

He was warned that his shortsightedness would affect future generations, but he continued in his selfish ways until his death. Do you know what happened next? As soon as he died, all of the good he had brought about died, too. The nation went right back to its sinful ways under the leadership of his son.

It's so easy for us to focus on the right now, especially during tough times. However, as we see with Hezekiah, that can have disastrous results. When Hezekiah's son Manasseh took over, he actually reestablished some of the idolatrous practices that his father had abolished.

If we focus on where we are right now, with no regard for the future, we will start going downhill, just as Hezekiah did. Every day that we spend focusing on the tough times that we are experiencing, instead of focusing on getting closer to God, we're falling further away.

Heavenly Father, forgive me of my sins and shortsightedness. I trust in your strength. I want to do only the things that please you, Lord.

56
Growing in Patience

Humble yourselves, therefore, under God's mighty hand,
that he may lift you up in due time. Cast all your anxiety on
him because he cares for you. (1 Peter 5:6-7, NIV)

f you want to run in a marathon race, you can't get in shape in one week. If you want to take the medical school exam, you can't get ready for it in one week. If you want to be a great golfer, you can't go out, take a few lessons, and be ready the next week. You have to prepare in your knowledge and skill day by day by day; build on it and increase in it.

"Lord, when are you going to do this?" "When is it going to happen?" These are natural questions, but Jesus said we don't need to know when. All we need to do is be ready. In Matthew 24, we read that the disciples were impatient and full of questions. They wanted to know when Jesus was coming again, and when his kingdom would be established.

And Jesus essentially replied: "You don't need to know that. Just be ready. Be on the alert. Nobody knows the day or the hour. You just be ready."

When we are in the midst of tough times, it is easy to cry out and ask God when the tough times will be over. When can we relax and breathe without fearing the next trouble that might arise? When can we just go on with our lives? But, you know, Jesus says we don't *need* to know when. All we need to do is trust in him. God has a glorious plan, and we are a part of it. Even the trials and tribulations that we encounter are a part of his plan; they are a part of our lives.

Understanding God's will, practicing it, and bearing fruit comes day by day by day by day. We build on knowledge and experience of the good times and tough times that we work through. Wait upon the Lord and depend on his strength.

Lord, forgive me for being impatient. Right this minute, I cast my anxiety on you. I know you care for me and you will lift me up in your perfect time.

57
God's Purpose

Whatever you do, whether in word or in deed, do it all in the name of the Lord Jesus, giving thanks to God the Father through him. (Colossians 3:17, NIV)

I n Paul's letter to the church at Colossae, he talked about God's purpose for humankind. Isn't it great to know this morning that God has a purpose for each of us? It doesn't matter what tough times we are facing; God has a special purpose for us. He knows all about our tough times. He even knows the number of hairs on our head. He has given every one of us a different thumbprint, and a special purpose unique only to us.

Have you opened your mailbox today? How many letters did you get addressed to "Occupant"? People don't even know who we are but they try to sell us something. We are living in a day and age of mass advertising. God is not, and never will be, in the mass advertising business. He's in the business of touching the lives of individual people.

God is working on fulfilling his purpose in our lives even during the tough times that we face. How we conduct ourselves—what we say, what we do—all of this works together to fulfill the purpose that God has for us. Anytime God gives us a purpose to carry out, he always supplies everything that we need to accomplish it. We don't have to go out and buy anything.

Look at Psalm 23. What does it say there? My cup is half filled? Or, 90 percent filled? No, it says "my cup runneth over!" (KJV). It overflows! According to Paul, God gives us "exceeding abundantly above" everything that we need to accomplish his plan for our lives (Ephesians 3:20, KJV).

When people see how we practice our faith, even in tough times, they will listen to what we have to say. One of the best keys of opening the door for Christian witness is when somebody sees the practice of walking worthy of the Lord. A lot of times, people don't believe what we say. They've got to see it before they will hear it. Transformed people can reveal God's power—steadfastness, patience, joy, and thanksgiving—to other people even in tough times.

Father, allow me to reveal your power to other people I meet today. Help me to show that even during the tough times, you are with me. You are my strength and my purpose in life. Thank you, Lord.

58
Temptation

I feel hopeless, and I cry out to you from a faraway land. Lead me to the mighty rock high above me. You are a strong tower, where I am safe from my enemies. Let me live with you forever and find protection under your wings, my God. (Psalm 61:2-4, CEV)

ear of tough times can paralyze the best of us, but it need not be that way for transformed people. Nothing that happens to us escapes God's notice. God is aware of and intimately involved in the details of our lives. He also promises that we will not be tested beyond our ability to respond.

Temptations are always strongest when we are in the middle of tough times. When our present looks bleak, Satan tries to tell us the future is going to be bleaker. He makes us feel alone in the midst of a crowd of people. He makes us feel distanced from the people who care for us and from the circumstances that we must face.

The truth in Ecclesiastes 4 speaks also to temptation. It says that two people teaming together are better than one who stands alone. If one of them falls [to temptation] the other can lift up his companion, but woe unto the one who falls if there's not another to lift him up, and if temptation can overpower him alone, two can resist temptation.

Transformed people need not feel alone. Wherever we are, God is with us. He is watching over us and will hold our hand if we ask him to. He is our very own strong tower that our enemies cannot climb. He welcomes us to the safety of his wing.

We can rise above the storm during tough times by keeping our focus on God.

Heavenly Father, thank you for not leaving me alone. Remove temptation from my pathway and hold my hand as we walk through the storm together.

59
A Gift of God

When God gives any man wealth and possessions, and enables him to enjoy them, to accept his lot and be happy in his work—this is a gift of God. (Ecclesiastes 5:19, NIV)

ob was the greatest man of all people in the East. He owned large numbers of livestock, and had many servants and children. He was a blameless and upright servant of God. Even God said that there was no man on earth like him. Job rejoiced in his blessings. Then in one fell swoop, this wealthy, upstanding man lost everything. He lost his oxen, his donkeys, his sheep, his camels, many of his servants—even his sons and daughters.

When confronted with all this devastation, what did Job do? He worshiped God. He didn't run from place to place and say "woe is me." He didn't grant a TV interview and ask when the government was going to help him. He turned his focus to God. Listen to what he said: "The Lord gave and the Lord has taken away; may the name of the Lord be praised" (Job 1:21, NIV).

God allowed Satan to test his humble servant time and time again. Job's wife and friends questioned his dilemma, and he suffered greatly. Finally, he was tested to the limit of his faith. As he began to complain and question God, the Lord called a halt to his suffering and rebuked him for questioning God's purpose.

Job praised God, saying, "'I know that you can do all things . . . things too wonderful for me to know. . . .' After Job had prayed for his friends, the LORD made him prosperous again and gave him twice as much as he had before" (see Job 42:1-10, NIV).

We can learn a lot from Job's story. There is a purpose in the tough times that we face, but only God knows what that purpose is. We need only to follow him and trust that he will reveal his plan to us when we need to know it.

O God, all my trust is in you. Erase temptation from my path and guide me throughout this day.